The Spiritual Life of Replicants

Murat Nemet-Nejat

The Spiritual Life of Replicants

Talisman House, Publishers
Greenfield, Massachusetts

Book designed by Samuel Retsov

Published in the United States of America by
Talisman House, Publishers
P.O. Box 896
Greenfield, Massachusetts 01032

ISBN-13: 978-1-58498-081-0

Cover illustration by Peter Hristoff, "Untitled" from "Ego Series" (2007).
Reproduced courtesy of the artist and C.A.M. Gallery, Istanbul.
Photo by Jean Vong.

"If you could see what I see with your eyes!"
>   *Blade Runner*, Nexus-6 Roy Batty addressing J.F. Sebastian, the
>   engineer who designed his eyes.

"And Enoch walked with God and was no more."
>   *Genesis, 5*

"You can only step into the same river twice."

Imagining death is before all image(-ining) the eye's absence

the absent soul tracing these transformations

"What cinematography means, writer of movement."
                    Stan Brakhage

ergo, death is the death of the cinematographer,

a writing of the eyes' movement disappearing,

its calligraphy

Burial of What Isseen in Silen c

Ray-ograph, a motion of light without the camera obscura, two photons colliding into each other.

The most intense form of silence is hearing,
as insomnia is the precarious longing for sleep,
eyes leading to blindness. I feel, old man,
seeingly, in the calligraphy of sudden thoughts.

Steam

Varnish evanescing pink
full of swe at beads   d a h m - a s k   burying

sweet bear ds   d u m b !   into -

swan and swarm birds   Muriel's

                                              burial -

horse and hazy   lazy ho urs seen

                  wall

(in cerulean blue tile   s oh seductive hot bath house)

soul

am   c l o u d o f m i s t i n n !

(solemn!) as   but not solo Jack!

                                                            scum

A bird flies a straight wide path in the eternal agitations of the sky, like a baby, sweet, its jewels showing.

The Theft

What death steals from us is our soul, the eluding traces of consciousness. In that respect, it is the mother fucker of all photographers, the paparazzi we must all endure, in our sixteen seconds of solitary fame.

Luc Godard Speaking Directly in *Masculin Féminin*

"Yes, in a way we are the center of the world —we speak with our lips, we see with our eyes, we think with our thoughts."

The Interviewee Should (De-)center Himself

"The interviewee should not look at the lens but at the other person asking the question, heard around the lens." (L. Godard)

Yet... yet, the ejaculatory force of the I,   my darling!

To L. C.

The whole thing is about sex, and the body's relation
to consciousness. You stay to my left
and listen to breathing. As he breathes
and you breathe, and you imagine a bird is flying in the room
And you tremble in anxiety, and think that
At the center where you are, at the umbilical facade
Of this room, which at first seems a library —
or its stacks — a loveliness is breathing
and the bird flying in the room
is reading all these books
to our exquisite regret & love's appreciation.
In this mathematical motion of consciousness
the room echoes in its own sounds.

What's for the eye must not duplicate what is for the ear… each being the rabbit chasing the other, **lead** leading the leader, against the tactics of speed, of noise, set the tactics of slowness.

A triangle entered the room,

with lips of a beast in distress —
crouched. I gazed
into it. Sweat
on my brow, I feared
the resilience of the coil

(uncoiling on three feet)

violent and more unpredictable
than the leap of a
warm panther.

I touched the lines
and caressed them.

The Triangle in the River

a triangle
            obfuscating
before rituals
of sleep
            insomniac's
delusions

in hardline
            geometry
let the stream swamp you
let let,
        oh how often!
blame me if I am onto you
triangle
            the angular
lunge of your arms
is a bill
        plucking

screams
it's axiomatic, the muzzled
dream

progressing only
under water

emerging
as waves,
            tsunami raves

lick the tip of your apex,
master-
bait
        outside the river

        In *Masculin Féminin* the audience knows everything about the noises outside the frame, the
        flow of the traffic, pin-ball clings, pop songs, etc.

An argument why she should turn from him to him

An argument why she should turn from him to him

An argument why she should turn from him to him

    e   m   n   e

F   I   N   I[1]

---

[1] In a pre-historic version of digital work, at the closing credits of *Masculin Féminin*, the letters f, i, n, I drop down from the word "feminine" in the middle of the screen, suggesting both an ending and infinity.

I and Godard have a crush on Karina
for Godard she exists,
I *think*.

"god, why hast thou forsaken me?"
"because *I* do not exist."

oh, i'less in Gaza!

no! hairless in Gaza.

A motion of light without the camera obscura, two entities pressing against each other.

The most intense form of silence is hearing,
as insomnia is the precarious longing for sleep,
eyes leading to blindness. I feel, old man,
seeingly, in the calligraphy of sudden thoughts.

The Mortal Proof

> Then the night rose up
> like a blackboard   *(blackbird escaping)*
>
> with a syllogism
> written in starlight.
>   Joe Donahue, *Terra Lucida*

I exist because I may cease to exist.

I *may* not exist; therefore I *am*.

A machine, image, if complex enough, will inevitably ask the question, am I mortal, or what *will* happen after I cease to exist.

Imagining its cessation is part of the essence of being conscious.

If the *future* exists
because it may cease to exist,
then death creates the idea of the future.

Is then the past only a memory chip,

disengaged from, at that *moment in the future,*
therefore we remember the past *towards* the moment of dying,
loosened chips from our decaying being,
floating to the sky

       in silent o o o's

like bubbles floating to the surface of water

Dying can be seen. But being dead, can't.

(Death is a winter whistle to the beauty of an earless forest)

w h e r e   t r e e s a r e f a l l i n g

there

what is   *not there*

is what's

what

no(t)w

"We need to confront vague ideas with clear images,"

which are thoughts.
the more elusive the connections among them
the clearer the thought

An image is a dialectic of a thought. Its *Replicant.*

eye

d

o

n

o

t

e

x

I

s

s

t

The camera steals our eyes to tell its own dreams. The parrot in my room talks to me,

affectionless

and vast.

The Mechanical Owl[2]

"An event can be a sweep of the eye, containing the colors of my daily living. " Stan Brakhage

---

[2] The mechanical owl sweeps from one end of the hall to another in *Blade Runner*, the pathos of the sweep of the eye attached to such a mechanical being.

"If the groom escapes out of the window the day of his wedding, he'll never come back." Gogol, *The Wedding*

Replicants

"A Phaesant lifts off and then disappears instantly among the trees, a porcupine buries in the tick underbrush, the dry leaves crackle as a snake slithers away. Not the encounter, but this flight of invisible animals is death   *as though*
                                         t."[3]

---

[3] This quote is from Giorgio Agamben's *Language and Death*. The last sentence of the quote, "Not the encounter, but this flight of invisible animals is thought," is altered.

The thoughts of disappearance *is*.

Disappearance *was*.

Thoughts of *was*

 is. is.

is is sang the bird.

in alternating shades.

How beautiful the color of tea
Is
In the morning
In the fresh air.
How beautiful
The fresh air
is.
How beautiful the young boy
Is.
How beautiful the tea
is.   (Orhan Veli)

I **hear**

w   w

  i   i

   n   n

    g   g

   s   s

     in   in

     the   the

     f   f

    o   o

   l   l

  i   i

 a   a

g   g

e   e

behind the wall.

the eye *sees* the contradictions in words and *sees* through itself, in an act of freedom.

The Wold Shadow
> "My laboriously painted vision of the god of the forest…. It had to do with the history of painting rather than any wood creature." Stan Brakhage[4]

you'll ascend the stairs slowly
on your skirts a golden pile of leaves
always you'll be looking at the East crying

Always looking at the East crying to be revived

waters are yellowing... your face paling in shadows
bending roses bleed bleeding to the ground
wait flame like on branches nightingale
has water burnt why is the marble bronze

From yellow to bronze to crimson to night is the fiery movement of the soul in its ascent.

Fire is reflected light in the evening twilight, soon to be replaced by the reflected light of the moon.

The nightingale and the branch on which it stands become one, waiting together.

wait flame like on branches nightingale

look at the crimson sky turning evening   (Ahmet Haşım)

---

[4] The quote is from Stan Brakhage's commentary in the DVD edition of his film *The Wold Shadow*. "Wold" is a Middle English word denoting a clearing in a forest —the space within which the shifts of light as the evening approaches might reveal the arrival of the gods of the forest. "Wold" also is a yellow derived from the roots of the plant "weld." The quote points to the linguistic roots of Brakhage's cinematic art, that whatever one's struggle against the materiality of things —of language— one is inevitably snared by it.

When One has given up One's life
The parting with the rest
Feels easy, as when Day lets go
Entirely the West

The Peaks, that lingered last
Remain in Her regret
As scarcely as the Iodine   (*the color of tea*)
Upon the Cataract.   (Emily Dickinson)

Windows, windows are better;
you see the birds passing by at least
instead of four walls.   (Orhan Veli)   *passes by*

The Eyes of Absence

Pursuing phantom pains.

Love of Words

A part of,
apart from my lover.

As words separate, I draw close
as words draw near, I fall apart.

The all sufficiency of language is a concept which, which can only be conceived by the all powerful.

So the creator Tyrell punished the glorious Nexus-6 models with mortality so that they do not learn too much and become like gods.

Without realizing that all the replicants arrived at was the weave wall of human emotions.

o

       o   scape

o

Cézanne painting with the same eye and the same soul a fruit dish, his son, the Montagne Saint-Victoire. *Equality of all things!* (R. Bresson)

The Still Life

The dusty roundness of the pot, the dandelion,
The pot, earth, covered by yellow foil, smoothly,
Each straining, dusty yellowness and shining foil,
To prune each other's color.

Nature

Condemned to a prison
of colors.

A mass of coffee grind's flying to the sky. A profound sadness is getting up,
about to get up, and leave, leaving behind its space
empty, that is, nothing to interpret
in its stead. Either for good or evil.

A portion of the universe waiting to be filled, is what's left.

Something has ended, you're relieved, have gotten rid of a burden.
(What the load is, I can't tell.)   (Seyhan Erözçelik)

the yellow of the carpet
lurks in the yellow of my eye.

and waits.

A dart's
instantaneous
license.

Photons Escaped

The perennial illusion is that the body is mortal, the soul immortal. The truth is that the body is immortal, endlessly involved in transformations, into dust, into humus, into water, into food chains... into star dust. What ceases to exist is the eye experiencing these transformations, the mind's eye, the soul, which is too too mortal, less durable than an electron.

Death is the ultimate moss
growing, morning
after.

I see, I see, said the blind man
to the deaf dog.

Reflected thoughts, at a
loss,
whisper in the forest

Flight Path of O's

Above reeds
the moon moaned
oysterless
for eight years

Loony
I swallow
the water.
with it
came
the moon,

full of oysters.

Luna

Last night the moon passed.
Passing out
it burst,
slaking
my thirst,
lit again
and left.

Tic

A sea
mussel am
I, ugly,
teaching
both lips
how
trembling
amorously
towards
the northern
in you my
love!

The floating vision of the god of water... darling! It had to do with the god of words, rather than any sea creature.

Through   darkly.   *tray*

    a wordless hole

                   pops out betrayal

Peter Petri

                         oh! promulgations!

Eda

If one wants to grasp the underlying principle of 20th century Turkish poetry in one stroke, it is that it brings animism into the middle of our global universe. Everything in that poetry becomes relatively clear from that perspective. Not only trees or animals, but in this poetry colors, objects, things, natural processes are in dialogue with each other, weaving their endless patterns. Eda is the structure of that pattern, the mesh of linguistic and geographic coordinates which go to its creation. Not the individual, but objects, colors, things are at the center of this endless transformation, the ego attached to it only tangentially, a detail, suffering and ecstatic. It is this peripheral relationship of consciousness to wider natural forces — subjective and objective, visceral and abstract — which gives Turkish poetry its stunning originality.

Consciousness dies, the eye dis-solves into motion, silhouetted by the dark matter of words.

r r
e   go   *d*

water mill why are you moaning
I am sad I am moaning
I fell in love with God
that's why I am moaning

my name is the sad box
my water flows over, lap lap
that's how my God wills
I'm sad I am moaning

They found me in a mountain
pruned my wings and arms
saw me fit for a water mill
am sad I am moaning

I am a mountain tree
neither sweet, nor bitter
to my God, prayerful
sad I am moaning

they severed from the hill my home
all my estate ruined
am a tireless poet
I'm sad I am moaning

all my sides pruned
set into place
this moaning comes from my Fair God
I'm sad I am moaning

I draw my water from low
spin pouring it above
see how I suffer God
sad I am moaning

Yunus arriving here doesn't laugh
no one reaches a goal
nothing in this mortality stands
I'm sad I am moaning   (Yunus Emre)

immense pool   O

              O

of sadness   o

            o

in an inner   o

       o

waveless   o   deep   boat/*boot*

       o

    because soundless

                        te

          because airless   i

                        d

O!   o

                        r

                        h

                      P

sundial's sandalled soundblast   A

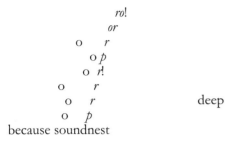

ro!
or
o   r
o p
o r!
o   r   deep
o   r
o   p
because soundnest

airless

O!   aphrodite

disappearance

Cast of Nexus-6 Characters in *Blade Runner*

Raechel (Sean Young) is an experimental replicant who believes she is a human

Roy Batty (Rutger Hauer), the leader, is a "combat model. " (Roy's master plan to meet his maker is hampered by the urgency created by his limited lifespan)

J. F. Sebastian, who is technically a human but, because of his Methuselah syndrome, falls into the spiritual state of a replicant.

Leon (Brion James), the youngest of the replicants. He still has two years to live.

Zhora (Joanna Cassidy). She is made of artificial snake scales… Her escape is structureless and fails, glasses crashing all around her —"*retires*[5] as an unarmed woman shot in the back"

Pris (Daryl Hannah). She joins Sebastian's army of human toys[6].

Hodge and Mary. Two fugitive replicants already *retired* before the movie begins, either by blade runners or the editor in the cutting room. They exist only as names.

---

[5] Retiring" is the euphemism blade runners use destroying (killing) a rebellious Nexus-6 android.
[6] Sebastian says the toys are his friends because he has made them.

Desire is dialectics
learning is enslavement
unlearning is *The Iliad* of our time
compelled by Achilles' rage of Patroclus

Ilium is a web site

My simple naked body, in its Sunday best,
implicit in the sealed coffin.
Farewell, farewell!

Poetry is ants crawling on the spine of my soul.

To Aishe[7]

Keep winged-ants in bottles
for ants wings are a minus
my writing is illegible like ants' prayers
modest as an ant
delicate like an ant's waist

full of ants - in pins and needles

---

[7] Aishe means "she who lives" in Arabic. Aishe was the third wife of Mohammad the prophet. Aishe echoes the name Raechel, the desired, second wife of Jacob.

Aishe's Wedding Ring

My heart
is melancholy

a red
stained
memory

hangs
on the

peach
tree.

Aishe Plays Speed Chess

Time turns around.
Your turn Aishe.

You can only step into the same river twice.

Auguries of Contradictions

how can a thought *that* does not exist not exist, *can not exist*, responding to a question?

If not exist, where's the question *provoking* it then…

The eye must *hear* its contradictions and see through itself —in an act of freedom.

As the parrot in my room talks to me, affectionless

and vast.

Questions and answers are mirrors reflecting each other's emptiness

where the eye travels.

Limbo

Descartes says the body is a machine.
Then a cyborg is a machine emulating a machine through organic pretensions, which Descartes disabuses us from.

The soul, the mechanical eye we are born with, stealing the body to tell its dream. *Then it dies, its specific mode of existence*, and it continues its wanderings to find another host. That's why the classical thinkers knew the ghosts of the dead wandered in the nether land —not searching for god, but yearning for another body.

Both soul and language are parasites in process in the unending flow of *things*, attached, loose emanating clicks[8], worm like sounds --surviving manna— but *nowhere*, nowhere the same.

---

[8] We arrive at Jack Spicer's paradisiacal clicks here.

love, of a not yet visible asia, is the barely sensible skin of plants.   (k. İskender)

The Turing Test

"If I disappear, would you come after me and hurt me?" (Raechel's question to Dekkar, the blade runner)

"can dreams be catching,
soul to soul?
shivering?
I'll warm you up."

AI

Would you love it
back,

as a mother?
it's easy to create

a child which would love you

Could you, *could you*, love someone programmed to say *yes*, to you, always, the inflatable slave   my darling?

The Methuselah Syndrome is not a disease of getting too old, but aging too fast.

"The toys are my friends. I made them." J. F. Sebastian, who suffers from the Methuselah Syndrome

Ode to a Triangle

A triangle with baby face

crawls on the ground to its mother.

its sharp snout
despite its inner ugliness

is beautiful to its mother

who gave it birth through Caesarean
to let the bulging points out.

The triangle nightmared of dying
it was sitting on a couch comfortable
and its mother was sleeping on the divan
suddenly it began to faint
it tried to wake up
its two bottoms rocked in the couch
its snout pressed
against the sides and folded back
but could utter
no sound
guttural clacking resounded within
itself
its mother slept on
rocked rocked to bring itself to
but its consciousness was menaced

the water of its world began to lower
and the triangle began to breathe again
it settled limply in its couch
its sweat falling down

The Triangle In Its Pure State
   "What a moth might see from birth to death —in a minute— if black were white and
   white black." S. Brakhage, *Mothlight*

dead
wing
crumbs

in its intense
self attraction
the triangle
cracks
like the one
who walked a crooked mile
smiling
dishes
out
different parts
of its face.

in the *V* of its legs
in the *Win g* side
the monkey at the doctor's office
(*the painting
came with the house*}
delouses
its happy brood.

the child's blue eye,
full of soap,

leans under
waits
for her clean
rubbing fingers
also full of soap.

the cockroach
at the corner
wanders.

the door opens,
shuts.

finger tips dry
all wrinkled.

When all is said and done, the Los Angeles of *Blade Runner* is a slum with deserted buildings and leaky roofs and constant rays of observing eyes as helicopter light penetrating through the holes and windows.

As the image is created with the arrival of light. The image arriving, as rays through cavernous cracks to your brain, is tyranny.

Repetition has a logic only the heart understands   and the tyrant exploits

The eye, silent, sexy, obedient
The silent, sexy, obedient
Sexy, obedient

The obedient, the eye — sexy, silent—
The eye, sexy, silent

The Andalusian Dog

The sliced eye
sees better.

Raechel's Walk (and a Few Quotes from Robert Bresson)

Raechel could not tell she was a replicant because she could not see herself walk. The sea of doll like anxiety in her heart, *that she was not real,* was purified by the short, toy like steps she took.

"The models[9] mechanized externally, internally free." R. Bresson

"The thing that matters is not what they show me but what they hide from me and, above all, *what they do not suspect is in them.*" R.Bresson.

"Don't run after poetry. It penetrates unaided through the joints" R. Bresson

---

[9] The "models" are the non-actors Bresson always required in his films to reveal his/hers/its essence in gestures.

Existence and Essence[10]

vertigo

balustrade

picnic.

the stairs the french garden
too wide, and of marble
the surface
chipped.
eye could not astraddle
sliding down them.

the picnic place
was cloistered
within flower beds
mother arranging the plates
along
the rectangular table
warned me
on and off
not to kick the ball too far.

once *eye* did.

the only moment could remember, and laughed
was when *Cousin George*
entered
trying to thwart with bare hands
the spurt of the fountain,
and slid in the wet pool.
going to it
legs up.
fell
we giggled
then put a hand on the mouth
in case *they* herd.

---

[10] To establish "emotional stability," Tyrell injects Nexus-6 models with memory chips. For that, in his own image, he uses his own past, a photo of his niece with her mother, etc. Dekkar the blade runner reveals to Raechel that she is a replicant by knowing the dream of her parents she keeps having without she telling him what that dream was. There is also a hint that Dekkar himself is a replicant because the detective Gaff, who is assisting Dekkar, seems to know Dekkar's dream of a unicorn. The replicants in the film seem to possess, and be possessed by, a single arch dream, a unified consciousness of an illusionary past.

returning, *we* all had our pictures
taken before the stairs

the white protuberance
behind.

eyne is the face in the corner
smudged
dirty.

Proof of Memory

a water flower
green circles
if you lift it
it will fall all limp
but in water
silent wires.
fish stroll
among them
poke their nose,
green turtle
doves
with wings.
once as a kid
our tent by the water
we camped for fish
a dry walk
and i was sent
to catch fish
with my bare hands.
my foot white
in water.
the sea weeds lolled
at my feet.
i
dove
but the fish that darted
was so big
at my nose.
i
ran back
as i saw its small tail
whip away.
i told my story
they laughed at me
all night long.

left foot
behind the ankle,
you shy
icon.

but I know
the shades
of whip marks
on your back.
you smeared
rouge
on your cheeks.
I smeared
rouge
on your ass.

in that motel
in Jamaica
a converted
old
plantation.

as you stretch your beautiful muscles in the air
you are shot
like a daffodil waking up.

your silhoutte folds,
against the window,
as Marlene Dietrich,
in the guise of a baritone, sings to me.

When Does Jesus Christ Become Truly Human?

When He doubts his divinity?

The heartless reassurances of the parakeet,
The pitiless wide eye of the owl.

At The Gates Of Heaven

"I was expecting you sooner."

"It's not easy to meet your maker."

"And what can I do for you?"

"Can the maker repair me?"

 "Would you like to be modified?"

"No. Stayed."

"What seems to be the problem?"

"Death…."

The future is born through caesarian of time,
into a lateral now, to which
we are the future.

"et tu, Caesar?"

Machines will conk out and being repaired, a few screws turned back,
will remember the very idea of non-being —an I-less wandering state—
Therefore, they will be our messengers from the underworld
or they too will not remember what happened

and waking up will ask, "where am I?"

The words "where am I," is this a supreme moment of being

a reference to sleep from almost the other side of sleep

(*Film Lumière*[11] eliminates space, telling a story twice, before and after it happened, in a simultaneous now.

The magnetic rosary vagrant thoughts create…

---

[11] Film Lumière is the form of this poem. See "Eleven Septembers Later: Readings of Benjamin Hollander's *Vigilance*," Murat Nemet-Nejat.

infinite gestures of finitudes.)

I.

The bell rings. "Oh, how are you" "I have not seen you for ages" "Come and have some coffee" "No I have to go. Why haven't you been calling me lately?" he goes to prepare coffee without answering. "I have been feeling awful lately. Depressed. And you know, Sana has been threatening to leave me." "Oh, I am sorry. Would you like milk with your coffee?" He does not answer. He puts in the milk. "You know she has begun to follow religious instructions. She goes to Shul every day. She has begun to wrap the bandanna I gave her for her birthday round her neck. But she won't shave her head. God damn it she won't. I read to her from Friday evening exhortations. No sugar thank you. About the obedience of women. You know, a good woman takes care of the camels and chattel of her husband. She should bend her neck." "Let me see, I don't know where the extra cup is." "You know she begins to wash dishes every time I read to her." "I know, I know. But give her time" "You know I am thinking of becoming a rabbi" "Well, it is better than becoming a priest. You don't read Dante any more" "But she won't leave me alone. I need peace for spiritual things. Do you think I should leave her?" "No, no, your woman is your first disciple." "I guess so. Let us keep in touch." "I'll call you next week."

II.

Sana does not have poetry in her soul. All she talks about is the price of celery in the stores. I don't care if she pays two cents more god damn it. She has this love of respectability. Do you know we wore wedding rings before we got married. Not that we saw anybody. You know the number of dinners we cancelled. She is sick or something. No, god damn it. Last time she broke a dish against the sink crying I want nobody here, I want nobody. So don't want anybody.

The Things Sana Made Ari Do

Get a new bed with real legs instead of a mattress. So he had to call the carpenter.

Buy a parakeet.

A dog. That was the only dog that didn't leave the house for two years.

Clean his nails.

Take a shampoo bath twice a week.

Not see his old girl friend and throw away all the pictures that belonged to her. Not the letters.

Some Things Ari Made Sana Do

Start religious instructions.

Remove the old paint crust from the window frames and make them loose.

Write.

III

A Poem That Ari Demanded That She Write

My husband is a skein of silence. You know he is a very attractive person. His beard, when washed and does not stink of tobacco, is as soft as lamb's wool. The first day we met, he spent half of the evening massaging his moustache in that easy chair I have grown to hate so much, and I sat in the couch. I thought he was mysterious. Suddenly he got up and held my hand. "You are sweet." "Yes, I am?" his gesture was mechanical like wound dolls. A miracle. He had entered my deepest thoughts. I was having carnal thoughts about him, thinking of the lips behind his beard, when suddenly he knew my sweetness.

Like a wired shark he embraced me. I was caught, caught by his sweetness, his blinding interest. My body was his and that's all that mattered.

His Chair

Chafed at the edges. Of overseating. The seat makes a hole. The headrest is filled with dandruff that regular brushing does not get rid of. Yellow, a grayish yellow... I will put doilies on the headrest and change it every week. But he calls it bourgeois. The back half of the seat shines with a gray yellow. Smooth, curving towards the center. A cigarette burn hole in the middle. One armrest, the one next to the pipe, is also shiny. That's where he keeps his new prayer books. But it is less smooth. Strips of the old design is still visible.

> a quiet life falls out of God's ear
> like manna, shining.

IV

The Parakeet Record To Teach It How To Talk

"Go down... Go down... To sleepp..." "No that's the flip side. Here now..." Twit, wit wit wit. Twit. Twit. Wit. Twit, twit, twit. Wit, wit. "I'm a parrakeet. I'm a parrakeet. Good morning. Good morning. Good morning." Twit. Wit. Wit. Wit. "I'm a parrakeet. Good morning. Good evening. Good evening."

"Now we are going to say a Ffew Worrds:

        Good morning   Good morning
        Good morning   Good morning

Now let's hear the parrakeet doo it:

        Good morning   Ghd mrnyng
        Good morning   Ghd mrnyng

Now let's hear your parrakeet do it:

        Good morning   ....
        Good morning   ....

"Say it you lousy parrakeet." (Good morning) "Say it or I'll wring your neck." "You are frightening the poor beast Ari."

        Good morning

"Say it bird. O.K. we'll put on the record again. Perhaps it needs to hear the parrakeet once more."

        Twit. Twit. Twit. Wit. Wit. Wit. Twit.

Don't sing I tell you. Talk. "Ari perhaps what we should do is leave on the record near its cage for the night." "What shall we do then stupid. We'll start talking like parrakeets before this dumb bird."

"... hear the parrakeet doo it:

        Good morning   Ghd mrnyng
        Good morning   Ghd mrnyng

V

From Ari's Short Story

A roomy bed. White walls. Ease, easeful mirth. The nurse's bracelet. "Do you want your pan now?" "I want to retch." "That is not till the afternoon." "I want to see the doctor." "He just saw you, but you were asleep. Your temperature is good." "I want to retch I said." "Then you must do it on your own. We have a shortage of staff you know." "Oh I am sorry."

The sorry twinkle of the window. "Give me your wrist" "No" "Yes my dear. Now don't be naughty"

She relinquished a fart when she knew she wasn't going to die.

"Hello, my name is Marvin... You look like a flower. May I hold your hand." He has a narrow strip on his skull where no hair grows. A birthmark. "Please, I need human contact, please. I'll sit next to your bed until you talk to me. You know the nurses won't bother me. It is the waiting hours. From 1:30 to 3:30. And I give them chocolate bars if you are silent and I want to wait a bit longer. I will make a nest here if I want to. A bird. I will be forever your faithful bird. Marvin the bird."

"Go away. what! Don't sit."

"He took me down to the beach and I had to follow him. I don't know why but I had to follow him. Sacrifice, he calls it. True loyalty, or whatever his bitchy teeth can express."

VI

Sana...

The holy bird of god out of the window. How it hovers. Dirty window. If I stretch my hand. But he should not see it. He lost me. The lousy Jew. His dirty beard. I hate his dirty beard. And his fucking hands, his fucking fucking hands. And his brown penis which is hard and elastic in the dark and he orders my hand to it, and I must suffer it in the dark, out of obedience, old faithfulness. But the bird is soft and white. Behind the dirty window. If I can reach it. When he is not. Yes he must not be here. But he won't see me. Because the dirty Jew is blind and makes me blind with his brown penis. He orders me to it. Hard and elastic. Then the sorry it, returns to its corner, shriveled the guilty thing. Then I can sleep. But then the embrace starts. "Darling, I am depressed. Hold me... You lousy bitch. Hold me." A cockroach is blind and peaceful. Sniffs the flaked walls of my bedroom. I'll pry open the window tomorrow. Don't worry.

The wings beat. Tche... tche... tche... "What?" "I am here now." "Without my slippers, I am coming. Don't wake him up. No, no."

VII

Ari's Climax

You are all woman. You are feminine. You are all thighs. You are mouth. Give me your mouth. I am your god. Give me your grapes. I want to suck them. Your clitoris. You are like a flower which I will enter. I will pour my ambrosia. Give me your flower. You are all thighs. You are all woman. Press your legs against me. Oh, you are all buttocks. You slave. Oh, pour your kisses into me. Kisses from your breast. I am a Greek god, drinking your ambrosia, licking it from your thighs. Give me your lips. I will swallow them. Lift yourself. Give me your thighs. I will press. Give me. Oh, my woman. You are all woman. Come my darling, come my pussycat. Come. Oh. Give me your thighs. You are all woman. Come come. You are all womb. All red. Like apples. Like a cup. I will pour my ambrosia into your cup. Then drink. Be god. Oh my goddess. Oh my goddess. Oh my slave, my thighs. Oh you are all thighs. How bumpy they are. Oh curve your hair. I will play with your hair. Oh give me your lips, lips, lips, I am coming, come come, darling. Ugh. I am coming. Come Ugh come. Ugh. Ugh. Cum darling cum. Ugh ugh ugh. Ghea, gheaaaa eeee...

VIII

Dear Murat. I am sending you this tape instead of a letter since, as I told you, I can not write. I can not put my thoughts on paper. Be careful since I paid a hundred bucks to have the background cleared. I took the tape before Sana's suicide so you'll hear her voice in it. It was the last time we joked together. It was at the end of the next week that she threw herself out of the window. You know you told me she was the calmest of my girl friends. The sanest. In a sense she was. She never talked. Sometimes we sat in the room. I felt depressed. My pipe was no use. I'd ask her to cheer me up. She never answered. She turned the pages of my newspaper. Most I got out of her was, "What do you want me to do?"

But what you will hear is a happy occasion. We listen to "4 O'clock Blues" which we both like so much... "River, I want the river." God damn it you stole these lines from me. Sana, shut up. I'll say what I want to my old friend here. I said these words to him and he uses them in a poem. Is that fair. Why don't you go to the other room. BizzX*&KNgd,.

Mary was a sweet lover
Her cunt was in the drawer
Birds prattled in her panties
Her loving was dementis. How do you like it Sana?

IX

The damn guy is impossible. Do you know one day he made me sit in a chair and read a whole damn short story, for one and a half hour, about this girl in a mental asylum, Karala, Aura, or something, who had attempted suicide. Murat, he says, listen to my story. Don't, if you can. He shoots this look at you. He is a real monster. So I sat next to him. After the fifth page I want to pee. "May I one minute." "… Yes." I sure disturbed his trance. I half peed outside the pot fearing to delay the thing too long. One day I would like to tell all these to him. Right to his face. I wonder how the poor girl lives with him. I must say she is the only one who doesn't complain. Is it because she is no intellect, even saying, "Murat, that man is driving me crazy." I don't even see it in her eyes. Ah, I was saying about the story. He continues reading it. I have already begun to sneak a look to the bottom of each page to see if the writing went on. God, for seventeen pages. "Well? What do you think?" "It's very interesting. Different from what you write today." "What?" "I say it's different from what you write today. What was that about the man tickling Aura's heel (it is Aura, isn't it) to stop her from puking?" "It wasn't a man it was a nurse. They do this in asylums. I'll leave you a copy of the whole story." "Oh thanks. Do you have enough copies?"

Then he directing me to his previous girl friend. "Go and see if she is alright. You know I'm afraid of Sana. She doesn't let me do anything in the house. Lower your voice! Don't answer me. She may wake up. We have a moment together alone"

"How is the bastard?" "The same" The mess of this house. Rattan bird cages. Wirings. Flower pots. Newspapers piling up. Weeks of *The New York Times*. "Come and sit down. Do you know what the bastard did to me. He made me bash my head against that bath tub. Lucky I had my wits about. Let us die intensely he says. I never saw him cut his finger even. Do you know the sign he carries on his key chain. His Phi Beta Kappa sign. He has his diploma on his wall. The mousy anti-bourgeois. I hear he has gone into religion now. Has he grown sausages round his temples yet. He sure stinks enough to be religious." "Please, I come with best wishes from him." "You are an asshole Murat. Utter asshole." "You don't want me to dignify..." "Come on come. I wish him well too. I hope he'll be the chief rabbi of the West Manhattan and half of the Bronx. May they bury him with his books." "Do you have a message for him?" "A message? Why not. Tell him I am very well. The best."

"Have an extra minute?" "Why?" "Sit a while" "I can't" "You fag you. Ari may have been insane, but he did have a cock." A light burned on the chest." "Why do you burn your candle in the middle of the day?" "Because I like it." "Do you know Ari told me you always had to have light at night." "So he did, eh, you messenger boy. Now shove off." "Good bye, I will relay your best wishes to him... You know he tells me he had his inspiration about religion from your candles" "Fucking go I said"

X.

This is a poem of exorcism. To exorcise a suicide out of my system. As though I was there. I pushed Ari's wife off the window. The woman in his story was his real lover. I don't remember her name. Aura. Carla. Karin. Something like that. A mulatto. Her skin was brown. He was full of suffering. He met her in a suicide in his imagination. Wrote a story about her and, one day, made me sit through twelve pages of shit glued to a chair. I couldn't move because he had an antenna for my every gesture. Even if I shifted my legs his gaze turned to me. Chased her around her bed. Sana was a mere faded picture whom he turned into art, into his madness. How the acid of his eyes engulfed everybody. His wife. Me. With his proud intensity. Claiming the last drop of sympathy. The peel of love. Now the hatred must blurt out after this exile of silence. Now that she is dead, he is dead too. The story is over.

I'll only remember rushing to the bathroom between pages and dripping half of my urine on the floor not to make him wait. But still I will make him wait. Wait for my telephone calls. He can have my praise, only my empty showers of glory on his story.

"I've seen things you people wouldn't believe. Attack ships on fire off the shoulder of Orion. I watched C-beams glitter in the dark near the Tannhauser Gate. All those moments will be lost in time, like tears in rain... Time to die." (The combat model, super replicant Nexus-6 Roy Batty addressing Dekkar, the blade runner who is pursuing him, just before it spares his life after reminding him it is not easy to live constantly in fear.)

The First Moment on the New Land

Terror like the wind of asphalt
In zero weather cockroach steps
A sun sinks drunk faint at the end
Of a drinking orgy —pale— reeling
Down the road. A dog begs shelter
From the wind thinking its howling
Another dog. A thousand ships
Swept to this island —called the cove
of the sun. The wind
Of white birds humbled them. Some drowned
Hurt by their beauty. A few licked
The frost off their bristles.

His thumb snapped off, he survived to the shore.
He ignored the beauty of the birds,
The mad music their white hair made
And the gray foam. He lost one thumb
Holding to the foremast in the cold.
One night in the last week of his trip
He had a dream. A bird was laughing at him,
Flying over its head, clacking its beak,
Truly laughing. His mother crept next to him.
He had not seen her for years, wandering
In the seas. Her hair was gray
As he knew her. She pushed her arm under
His head but his neck was stiff, staring
Staring at the bird. It cackled. Then she
Disappeared. He opened his eyes. The gray water.

It was next week that the first weeds
Appeared floating on the surface. Birds, not followers
Of garbage from the ship, but new birds
Of land, flew, made circles at a distance.
They did not land on the ship.

The first seen landscape was sand. For
Some reason, the snow did not reach the shore
But stopped on the side of the first dunes.
He dug the sand until he reached the rock
And buried his only possession under. Then,
Crouched against the dune, he outwore the day.

Terror, like the wind of asphalt, swept.
The sun, faint, fell

Behind the hill. Left a sheen of red,
Like his mother's copper pots, for a moment
on the water.

A Few Thoughts on Fragments

I.

The poem *The Spiritual Life of Replicants* is infused with Sufi ideas, and this infusion results in a poetry that consists of movements of thought in a visual field. The reader experiences the movements as he or she is ensnared by them reading the poem. The thought patterns are arabesque, circuitous, tangential, reflecting the Sufi sense that reality is not stared at directly; but it can only be touched, glimpsed at reflectively, as fragments, the way, for instance, the reality of the wind can be seen (or heard) in the traces it leaves on the movements of branches. In this way the infinite—the invisible, the music of silence—descends to visibility.

The primary struggle for the poet in *The Spiritual Life* is to create a spectacle in which words, language can act freely, following impulses inherent in them—basically, each page becoming a scene in which, in different constellations, words enact their drama. The primary unit in this enactment is the fragment. A fragment is like a lyric poem or an epigram in length, but is devoid of any lyric persona (no lyric I), replacing it in the poem with the "mechanical eye" of a lens. In the process, the distinction between human and non-human, organic and non-organic, thought and sensation disappears, enabling fragments to move "across party lines."

Fragments are thoughts afloat.

Fragments function almost completely without metaphors. They are replaced by gestures. A gesture is a sensory observation, a riff of thought which is complete in itself; in this completeness, it lures the reader into itself (every love starts with attraction), making the poem possible. Nevertheless, a fragment also desires complementation by opening up to and reacting with other ones. In this interaction, fragments create the very field of energy, the spectacle within which the drama of language occurs. This paradox reflects the Sufi consciousness where the human is embedded in its physical being—and the chains of its language—and burns with the desire for a greater union.

Walter Benjamin states in one of his fragments, "Language has made unmistakably plain that memory is not an instrument for exploring the past, but rather a medium. It is the medium of that which is experienced, just the earth is the medium in which ancient cities lie buried. He who seeks to approach his own buried past must conduct himself like a man digging."[1] Given that *The Spiritual Life* is the buried city, written at a specific time in the past with specific constellations of fragments, the reader is put in a special place. He/She can not remain passive before this medium, but must start digging from his/her place in the present. Constellations may move and rearrange themselves. Nevertheless, hopefully, as a result, the poem—itself a fragment[2]—will open itself up, being complemented by the community surrounding it.

II. Eda and Cinema

> "A poetry where meaning has turned into pure motion created by the movement of the eye on the printed page, a spiritual filmic language…"

Eda is a poetics of Sufism embodied in the structure of the Turkish language. This linguistic quality —thought not as statements, but thought as a linguistic tissue—is achieved in Turkish primarily through its syntax:

---

[1] *Walter Benjamin's Archive*, "Excavation and Memory," translation by Esther Leslie (Verso, 2007), p. I.
[2] *The Spiritual Life of Replicants* constitutes Part VI of a seven-part poem "The Structure of Escape."

Turkish is an agglutinative language, that is to say, declensions occur inside the words as suffixes. Words need not be attached to either end of prepositions to spell out relationships, as in English. This quality gives Turkish total syntactical flexibility. Words in a sentence can be arranged in any permutable order, each sounding natural.

The underlying syntactical principle is not logic, but emphasis: a movement of the speaker's or writer's affections. Thinking, speaking in Turkish is a peculiarly visceral activity, a record of thought emerging. The nearer the word is to the verb in a sentence, which itself has no fixed place in the sentence, the more emphasis it has. This ability to stress or unstress —not sounds or syllables; Turkish is syllabically unaccented— but words (thought as value-infested proximity) gives Turkish a unique capability for nuance, for a peculiar kind of intuitive thought.

—*Eda: An Anthology of Contemporary Turkish Poetry*, Talisman House, Publishers, 2004, pp. 5/6

The "I" experiencing phenomena and phenomena themselves disappear and unite in an animistic synthesis. The "I" becomes the "eye" merging with it in an open-ended weave of language.

The same dissolution occurs also in Sufism. Sufism is the dissolution —even destruction— of the self in ecstatic suffering.

If one considers *The Spiritual Life* an attempt to translate the flexibility of Eda, the spiritual universe of Sufism into English, one sees the antagonist the poet must encounter: the nearly absolute inflexibility of the English syntax. English turns into a prison within which Eda must move and, more importantly, from which it must escape. The spectacle-ization of the poem in *The Spiritual Life*, fragments becoming basic poetic units, is the path to achieve that goal.

Placed in proximity in fluid, tangential combinations, fragments misfit together, rather than perfectly synchronize. The jagged connections energize the reader to jump across, therefore, making the reader an active participant in the creation of meaning in the poem. The reading often involves his or her eye tracing the mechanical eye —a panning lens— buried in the sinuous, meandering movements of the poem. In this interaction between "human" and "machine"—"silhouetted by the dark matter of words."—thoughts dissolve into space, into motion and light.

"In *The Spiritual Life of Replicants* Heraclitus meets Ridley Scott on the *Blade Runner* set and they both go off to have tea with John Cage. In this impressive poem Murat Nemet-Nejat carefully sets fragment against fragment, word against word, idea against idea. Meaning collides and colludes with language itself. The result is at times dizzying, always dazzling." —Christopher Sawyer-Lauçanno

"The space already emptied on the page: here a space always already of potential, preceding existence, the thing/sight itself.

"And existence as a modality: what if the world were the world? Murat explores, peels back, on the verge of extinction; the verge disappears against the nub of the real, the eye.

"Eda, and what exists as if there were a reading to be given of the world which retreats, retracts any, and any such.

"Fragments—fallen to the bottom of the page, but annealed by white, by the absence of things hardened by consciousness and the generation of meaning. So always closer to suicide, deicide, the two identical. Then the brightness of replicants: among us we are all constructed.

"A fragment as thought without genealogy, or rather, nothing *but* genealogy. And replicants, as fragments among languages, ec/statics—" *—Alan Sondheim*

"In *The Spiritual Life of Replicants*, itself part of a longer poem of many sections called "The Structure of Escape," Nemet-Nejat orchestrates a Feuilletton thriller in which investigations of the human/replicant and spiritual eye/I are conducted against the backdrop of a dramatic linguistic prison breakout. Taking the path opened by the flexible fragments-as-units of Turkish syntax and the embrace of Eda, the poet & poem involve the visceral participation of the reader in a struggle to escape the inflexible, imprisoning lockdown of English syntax into which, paradoxically, the poet is translating his flexible Turkish syntax and visionary sense of Eda. Inviting, urging, the reader to join in the action, *The Spiritual Life of Replicants* dramatizes the act of reading itself as a struggle for and of Liberation on many fronts, in which the merging of hunter and hunted, replicant/machine and human, human and deity, reader and poet occurs." *—David-Baptiste Chirot"*

Poet, translator and essayist, **Murat Nemet-Nejat**'s edited and largely translated *Eda: An Anthology of ContemporaryTurkish Poetry* (2004), translated Orhan Veli, *I, Orhan Veli* (1989), Ece Ayhan, *A Blind Cat Black and Orthodoxies* (1997), and Seyhan Erözçelık, *Rosestrikes and Coffee Grinds* (2010). He is the author of *The Peripheral Space of Photography* (2004) and, recently, the memoir/essay "İstanbul Noir" (2011), the poems "steps" (2008), "Prelude" (2009), "I Did My Best Work During a Writer's Block" (2009), "Disappearances" (2010) and "Alphabet Dialogues/Penis Monologues" (2010). He is presently working on the long poem "The Structure of Escape."